LIFE STORIES / BIOGRAFÍAS

HARRIET TUBMAN

Gillian Gosman

Traducción al español: Eduardo Alamán

PowerKiDS press

New York

Published in 2011 by The Rosen Publishing Group, Inc.
29 East 21st Street, New York, NY 10010

First Edition

Editor: Jennifer Way   Spanish translation: Eduardo Alamán
Book Design: Ashley Burrell and Erica Clendening

Photo Credits: Cover (background), p. 13 Charles H. Phillips/Time & Life Pictures/Getty Images; cover (inset), pp. 12, 18–19 MPI/Getty Images; pp. 4–5, 21, 22 (left) Library of Congress; pp. 6–7 Jupiterimages/Getty Images; pp. 8–9 Wikipedia Commons; p. 9 SuperStock/Getty Images; p. 10 SSPL/Jamie Cooper/Getty Images; pp. 10–11 Time & Life Pictures/Mansell/Getty Images; p. 14 Fotosearch/Getty Images; pp. 15, 22 (right) Hulton Archive/Getty Images; p. 16 Marvin Joseph/The Washington Post/Getty Images; p. 17 Debbie Egan-Chin/NY Daily News Archive/Getty Images; p. 18 Heritage Library Foundation; p. 20 Ira Block/National Geographic/Getty Images.

Library of Congress Cataloging-in-Publication Data

Gosman, Gillian.
[Harriet Tubman. Spanish & English]
Harriet Tubman / by Gillian Gosman. — 1st ed.
    p. cm. — (Life stories = Biografías)
Includes index.
ISBN 978-1-4488-3220-0 (library binding)
1. Tubman, Harriet, 1820?-1913—Juvenile literature. 2. Slaves—United States—Biography—Juvenile literature. 3. African American women—Biography—Juvenile literature. 4. African Americans—Biography—Juvenile literature. 5. Underground Railroad—Juvenile literature. I. Title.
E444.T82G67618 2011
973.7'115092—dc22
[B]

2010036803

Web Sites: Due to the changing nature of Internet links, PowerKids Press has developed an online list of Web sites related to the subject of this book. This site is updated regularly. Please use this link to access the list:
www.powerkidslinks.com/life/tubman/

Manufactured in the United States of America
CPSIA Compliance Information: Batch #WW11PK: For Further Information contact Rosen Publishing, New York, New York at 1-800-237-9932

CONTENTS

Meet Harriet Tubman 4
Young Araminta Ross 6
Slavery in America 8
To Freedom! 10
The Guide 12
Tricks of the Trade...14
The Underground Railroad 16
Abolitionist and Union Hero 18
The End of the Line 20
Timeline 22
Glossary 23
Index 24

CONTENIDO

Conoce a Harriet Tubman 5
Los primeros años... 7
Esclavitud 9
¡El camino a la libertad! 11
La guía 13
Trucos 15
El Ferrocarril Subterráneo 17
Heroína abolicionista y del ejército de la Unión 19
El final de la línea 21
Cronología 22
Glosario 23
Índice 24

Meet Harriet Tubman

Harriet Tubman is sometimes called the Moses of her people. Moses is a figure in the Bible. In the Bible, Moses leads his people, the Hebrews, from **slavery** to **freedom**.

In her lifetime, Harriet Tubman led many African-American slaves from the South to freedom in the North. In doing so, she became a part of American history.

Tubman changed her first name. During her childhood, she was known as Araminta. As an adult, she went by Harriet.

Conoce a Harriet Tubman

A Harriet Tubman se le conoce como la Moisés de su pueblo. Moisés es un personaje de la Biblia. En la Biblia, Moisés conduce a su pueblo, los hebreos, de la **esclavitud** a la **libertad**. Harriet Tubman llevó a muchos esclavos afro-americanos del sur a la libertad en los estados del norte. Por eso, Tubman tiene un lugar en la historia de los Estados Unidos.

Tubman cambió su nombre de pila. Durante su infancia, era conocida como Araminta. En su edad adulta lo cambió a Harriet.

Young Araminta Ross

Harriet Tubman was born around 1820. Her name at birth was Araminta Ross. Young Araminta was a slave on a Maryland **plantation**, or farm. She worked both in the house and the fields.

When Araminta was a teenager, she tried to keep another slave from being hurt by an angry **overseer**. The overseer threw a weight that hit Araminta in the head. The injury troubled her for the rest of her life.

This map shows the United States around 1820. Maryland is shown in red.

Este mapa muestra a los Estados Unidos en 1820. Maryland está en rojo.

Cotton was one of the South's most important crops. These people are slaves and are picking cotton on a southern plantation.

El algodón era uno de los cultivos más importantes del sur. Estas personas son esclavos y están recogiendo algodón en las plantaciones del sur.

Los primeros años

Harriet Tubman nació alrededor de 1820. Su nombre al nacer era Araminta Ross. Araminta era esclava en una **plantación**, o granja, de Maryland. Araminta trabajaba en la casa y en el campo.

Cuando Araminta era joven, trató de evitar que un **capataz** lastimara a un esclavo. El capataz arrojó una pesa a la cabeza de Araminta. La lesión afectó a Tubman el resto de su vida.

SLAVERY IN AMERICA

Harriet Tubman lived during a time in which slavery was **legal** in the South. Businesses in the North made goods using southern crops. In this way, all of America had a part in slavery.

Abraham Lincoln believed slavery was wrong. When he became president in 1860, 11 Southern states **seceded** from, or left, the nation. This was how the **Civil War** began.

CONFEDERATE STATES OF AMERICA

This map shows the Southern states that seceded from the United States in red. These states formed the Confederate States of America.

Este mapa muestra en rojo a los estados del sur que se separaron de los Estados Unidos. Estos estados formaron los Estados Confederados de América.

Abraham Lincoln was president of the United States throughout the Civil War. The war lasted from 1861 until 1865.

Abraham Lincoln fue presidente de los Estados Unidos durante la Guerra Civil. La guerra duró de 1861 a 1865.

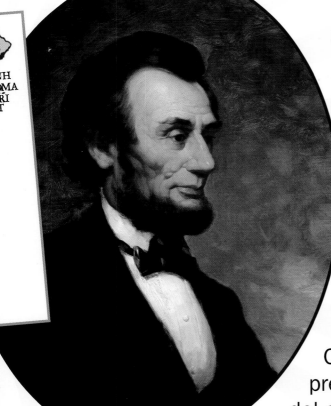

ESCLAVITUD

Tubman vivió durante una época en la que la esclavitud era **legal** en los estados del sur. Además, las empresas de los estados del norte hacían mercancías usando los cultivos del sur. De esta manera, todos los estados jugaban un papel en la esclavitud.

Abraham Lincoln creía que la esclavitud era un error. Cuando Lincoln fue elegido presidente en 1860, 11 estados del sur se separaron del resto del país. La **secesión** de los estados del sur provocó la **Guerra Civil**.

To Freedom!

In 1844, Harriet married John Tubman. John was a free black man. Harriet was still a slave. In 1849, there was talk on the plantation that some slaves would be sold, including Harriet. She could be sold to a master who lived far away.

Harriet decided to run away. She left on foot in the middle of the night. She made her way north and settled in Philadelphia, Pennsylvania.

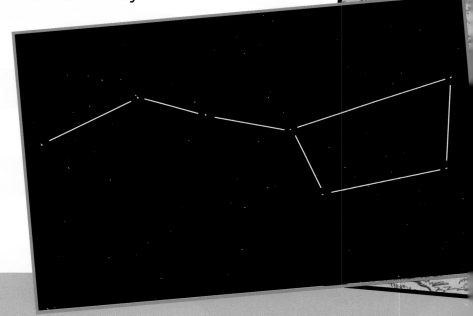

The group of stars shown here is the Big Dipper. The Big Dipper helped point Tubman and other runaway slaves north.

Este grupo de estrellas es la Osa Mayor. La Osa Mayor ayudó a que Tubman y otros esclavos fugitivos se orientaran en su camino hacia el norte.

Runaway slaves faced many dangers. As shown in this drawing, they might be caught and shot at or even killed.

Los esclavos fugitivos enfrentaban muchos peligros. Como se ve en este dibujo, podían ser apresados y fusilados, e incluso asesinados.

¡EL CAMINOA LA LIBERTAD!

En 1844, Harriet se casó con John Tubman. John era un negro libre. Harriet todavía era esclava. En 1849, en la plantación, se hablaba de que algunos esclavos, incluyendo a Harriet, serían vendidos. Harriet podría ser vendida a un terrateniente que viviera muy lejos.

Harriet decidió huir. Harriet escapó a pie durante la noche. Harriet caminó hacia el norte y se estableció en Filadelfia, Pensilvania.

THE GUIDE

In 1850, Harriet Tubman went back to Maryland to help her sister and her sister's two children escape from slavery. After she did that, she led her brother and two friends to freedom.

She made a third trip in 1851, this time to bring her husband north. When she got to Maryland, she learned that John had married another woman. She then made the trip north with slaves who wanted to escape.

Here is Tubman (far left) around 1885 with some of the people she helped bring to freedom.

Aquí vemos a Tubman (izquierda), alrededor de 1885, con algunas de las personas a las que llevó a la libertad.

This picture shows people helping a group of runaway slaves make their way to freedom.

Esta foto muestra a la gente ayudando a un grupo de esclavos fugitivos en su camino a la libertad.

La guía

En 1850, Harriet Tubman regresó a Maryland para ayudar a su hermana y sus sobrinos a escapar de la esclavitud. Más tarde ayudó a su hermano y a dos amigos.

Tubman hizo su tercer viaje en 1851 para llevar a su esposo al norte. Al llegar a Maryland, Tubman se enteró de que John se había casado con otra mujer. Entonces, Tubman ayudó a otros esclavos a obtener su libertad.

TRICKS OF THE TRADE

Over time, Harriet Tubman led about 300 slaves to freedom. To do so, she had to be brave and smart.

She learned how to outthink the slave owners. Slave owners put ads in newspapers offering rewards for runaway slaves. Newspapers printed these ads on Mondays. Harriet began her trips north with escaping slaves on Saturday nights. This gave the runaway slaves a head start.

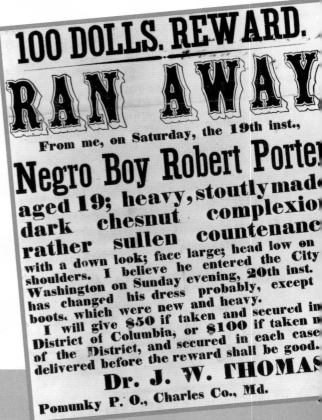

100 DOLLS. REWARD.

RAN AWAY

From me, on Saturday, the 19th inst.,

Negro Boy Robert Porter aged 19; heavy, stoutly made, dark chesnut complexion, rather sullen countenance, with a down look; face large; head low on shoulders. I believe he entered the City of Washington on Sunday evening, 20th inst. has changed his dress probably, except boots, which were new and heavy.

I will give $50 if taken and secured in District of Columbia, or $100 if taken out of the District, and secured in each case delivered before the reward shall be good.

Dr. J. W. THOMAS

Pomunky P. O., Charles Co., Md.

This is a newspaper ad offering a reward for the return of a runaway slave.

Éste es un anuncio de periódico ofreciendo una recompensa para quien regresara a un esclavo fugitivo.

14

Tubman said that she never lost a runaway on any of her trips north.

Tubman dijó que nunca perdió a un fugitivo en sus viajes al norte.

TRUCOS

Con el tiempo, Tubman llevó a cerca de 300 esclavos a la libertad. Para lograrlo, Tubman, tuvo que ser valiente y muy inteligente. Tubman aprendió a pensar antes que los dueños de los esclavos. Los dueños de los esclavos solían poner anuncios en los periódicos ofreciendo recompensas a quien regresara a los fugitivos. Estos anuncios se publicaban los lunes. Harriet comenzaba sus viajes al norte los sábados por la noche. Esto le daba una ventaja a los esclavos fugitivos.

The Underground Railroad

The network, or group of people, who helped runaway slaves travel north became known as the **Underground Railroad**. Tubman was one of the Underground Railroad's most famous conductors, or guides.

On the Underground Railroad, runaway slaves might hide in cellars. They might travel many miles (km) on foot. It was a long and dangerous trip. Conductors like Tubman helped them.

Many stops on the Underground Railroad were hidden within houses like this one in Maryland.

Muchas paradas del ferrocarril subterráneo se ocultaban dentro de casas como ésta en Maryland.

This house was an Underground Railroad stop. It has a secret tunnel that goes to the cellar of another house.

Esta casa era parte del Ferrocarril Subterráneo. En la casa hay un túnel secreto que va a la bodega de otra casa.

EL FERROCARRIL SUBTERRÁNEO

A la red de personas que ayudaban a los esclavos fugitivos se le conoce como el **Ferrocarril Subterráneo**. Tubman fue una de las guías más famosas del Ferrocarril Subterráneo. En el Ferrocarril Subterráneo los esclavos podían esconderse en bodegas. Podían viajar muchas millas (km) a pie. Era un viaje largo y peligroso, pero los guías como Tubman les ayudaban en su jornada al norte.

17

ABOLITIONIST AND UNION HERO

In the 1850s and early 1860s, Tubman began to work with **abolitionists**. Abolitionists spoke out against slavery and worked to make it illegal. Tubman spoke out with them.

When the Civil War began, in 1861, Tubman took jobs as a nurse, a cook, and a **spy** for the North. During her service with the Union army, she met a **soldier** named Nelson Davis. The couple married in 1869.

Tubman was a soldier and a spy for the Union army. She helped lead the 1863 raid on the Combahee River, in South Carolina, shown here.

Tubman fue soldado y espía en el ejército de la Unión. Tubman ayudó en el ataque del río Combahee, en Carolina del Sur en 1863, que se muestra aquí.

Abolitionists started newspapers, such as *The Liberator*. These newspapers spread news related to the abolitionist cause.

Los abolicionistas fundaron periódicos, como *El Libertador*. Estos periódicos difundían noticias relacionadas con la causa abolicionista.

Heroína abolicionista y del ejército de la Unión

En la década de 1850 y principios de 1860, Tubman comenzó a trabajar con los **abolicionistas**. Los abolicionistas se pronunciaban en contra de la esclavitud y buscaban hacerla ilegal.

Al inicio de la Guerra Civil, en 1861, Tubman trabajó como enfermera, cocinera y **espía** para los estados del norte. Durante su servicio con el ejército de la Unión, Tubman conoció a un **soldado** llamado Nelson Davis. La pareja se casó en 1869.

THE END OF THE LINE

After the Civil War ended, Tubman and her family moved to Auburn, New York. She spoke out in favor of women's rights, such as the right to vote. Tubman died, at the age of 93, on March 10, 1913.

Tubman is a true American hero. She put her life in danger so that people could enjoy freedom.

This is Tubman's home in Auburn. In 1908, she opened a home for elderly African Americans. She moved into this home in 1911.

Ésta es la casa de Tubman en Auburn. En 1908, Tubman fundó una casa para los ancianos afro-americanos. En 1911 se mudó a esta casa.

Tubman spoke out in favor of women's right to vote.

Tubman apoyó el derecho al voto de las mujeres.

El final de la línea

Después de la Guerra Civil, Tubman y su familia se mudaron a Auburn, Nueva York. En Auburn, Tubman habló a favor de los derechos de las mujeres, tales como el derecho al voto. Tubman murió el 10 de marzo 1913, a la edad de 93 años.

Tubman es una verdadera heroína de la historia estadounidense. Tubman puso su vida en peligro para que muchas personas pudiesen disfrutar de su libertad.

Timeline / Cronología

Circa 1820 / 1820 [aprox]

Harriet Tubman is born in Maryland. Her name at birth is Araminta Ross.

Nace Harriet Tubman en Maryland. Su nombre al nacer es Araminta Ross.

1844

Araminta Ross marries John Tubman. She changes her name to Harriet Tubman.

Araminta Ross se casa con John Tubman. Cambia su nombre a Harriet Tubman.

1849

Harriet Tubman escapes to the North.

Harriet Tubman escapa hacia el norte.

March 10, 1913 / 10 de marzo de 1913

Harriet Tubman dies.

Harriet Tubman muere.

1861–1865

The Civil War is fought. Harriet Tubman works as a nurse, soldier, and spy.

Se lleva a cabo la Guerra Civil. Harriet Tubman trabaja como enfermera, soldado y espía.

1850s

Tubman is a conductor on the Underground Railroad.

Tubman es conductora en el ferrocarril subterráneo.

Glossary

abolitionists (a-buh-LIH-shun-ists) Men and women who worked to end slavery.

Civil War (SIH-vul WOR) The war fought between the Northern and the Southern states of America from 1861 to 1865.

freedom (FREE-dum) The state of being free.

legal (LEE-gul) Allowed by the law.

overseer (OH-ver-see-ur) A person who watches over workers.

plantation (plan-TAY-shun) A very large farm where crops are grown.

seceded (sih-SEED-id) Withdrew from a group or a country.

slavery (SLAY-vuh-ree) The system of one person "owning" another.

soldier (SOHL-jur) Someone who is in an army.

spy (SPY) Someone who watches secretly.

Underground Railroad (UN-dur-grownd RAYL-rohd) A system set up to help slaves move to freedom in the North.

Glosario

abolicionistas (los/las) Los hombres y mujeres que trabajaron para acabar con la esclavitud.

capataz (el/la) Una persona que supervisa a los trabajadores.

esclavitud Un sistema en el que una persona que se considera "propiedad" de otro.

espía (el/la) Alguien que ve en secreto.

Ferrocarril Subterráneo (el) Un sistema creado para ayudar a los esclavos a obtener su libertad en los estados del norte.

Guerra Civil (la) Guerra entre los estados del norte y los estados del sur de 1861 a 1865.

legal Permitido por la ley.

libertad (la) El estado de ser libre.

plantación (la) Una granja muy grande donde se cultiva.

secesión (la) Separarse de un grupo o un país.

soldado (el) Alguien que está en un ejército.

Index

B

birth, 6, 22

C

Civil War, 8, 18,
   20, 22

F

freedom, 4, 12,
   14, 20

H

head, 6
Hebrews, 4

I

injury, 6

L

Lincoln,
   Abraham, 8

M

Moses, 4

N

name, 6, 22
North, 4, 8, 18,
   22

P

plantation, 6, 10
president, 8

S

slavery, 4, 8, 10,
   12, 18
slave(s), 4, 6, 10,
   12, 14, 16
soldier, 18, 22
South, 4, 8
spy, 18, 22

Índice

C

cabeza, 7

E

esclavitud, 5, 9,
   13, 19
esclavo(s), 5, 7,
   11, 13, 15, 17
espía, 19, 22

G

Guerra Civil, 9, 19,
   21–22

H

hebreos, 5

L

lesión, 7
libertad, 5, 13,
   15, 21
Lincoln,
   Abraham, 9

M

Moisés, 5

N

nacer, 7, 22
nombre, 7, 22
norte, 5, 9, 19, 22

P

plantación, 7, 11
presidente, 9

S

soldado, 19, 22
sur, 5, 9